COAST GUARD

Simon Rose

MEDIA ENHANCED BOOKS
AV2 BY WEIGL™
ADDED VALUE • AUDIO VISUAL

www.av2books.com

AV² provides enriched content that supplements and complements this book. Weigl's AV² books strive to create inspired learning and engage young minds in a total learning experience.

Your AV² Media Enhanced books come alive with...

Audio
Listen to sections of the book read aloud.

Key Words
Study vocabulary, and complete a matching word activity.

Video
Watch informative video clips.

Quizzes
Test your knowledge.

Go to www.av2books.com, and enter this book's unique code.

Embedded Weblinks
Gain additional information for research.

Slide Show
View images and captions, and prepare a presentation.

BOOK CODE

L 8 9 5 1 1 8

AV² by Weigl brings you media enhanced books that support active learning.

Try This!
Complete activities and hands-on experiments.

... and much, much more!

Published by AV² by Weigl
350 5th Avenue, 59th Floor
New York, NY 10118
Website: www.av2books.com   www.weigl.com

Library of Congress Cataloging-in-Publication Data
Rose, Simon, 1961-
 Coast Guard / Simon Rose.
    p. cm. -- (U.S. Armed Forces)
 Includes index.
 Audience: Grades 4 to 6.
ISBN 978-1-61913-630-4 (hbk. : alk. paper) -- ISBN 978-1-61913-631-1 (pbk. : alk. paper)
1. United States. Coast Guard--Juvenile literature. I. Title.
 VG53.R67 2013
363.28'60973--dc23   2012021995

Printed in the United States of America in North Mankato, Minnesota
1 2 3 4 5 6 7 8 9 16 15 14 13 12

062012
WEP170512

Project Coordinator: Aaron Carr
Design: Mandy Christiansen

Every reasonable effort has been made to trace ownership and to obtain permission to reprint copyright material. The publisher would be pleased to have any errors or omissions brought to their attention so that they may be corrected in subsequent printings.

Weigl acknowledges Getty Images as its primary image supplier for this title.

CONTENTS

WHAT IS THE COAST GUARD?

The Coast Guard is one of the main branches of the United States Armed Forces. The other branches are the Army, the Air Force, the Marine Corps, and the Navy. The Coast Guard is the main **maritime** safety and security force of the United States military. Maritime means having to do with the sea. The Coast Guard is the only branch of the military responsible for law enforcement on water.

The Coast Guard is part of the Department of Homeland Security. This department is in charge of keeping the United States safe from **terrorism**. It also makes sure that the United States is ready to deal with natural disasters, such as hurricanes and earthquakes. The president of the United States can place the Coast Guard under the control of the U.S. Navy at any time. The Coast Guard has more than 42,000 people on full-time active duty and about 8,000 part-time personnel in the **Coast Guard Reserve**. It also has about 30,000 members who help out as volunteers when needed. They belong to the **Coast Guard Auxiliary**.

★ The Coast Guard enforces the laws of the United States that have to do with the sea. This includes protecting the nation's ports.

STRUCTURE OF THE U.S. ARMED FORCES

Marine Corps

Army

Air Force

Navy

Coast Guard

National Strike Force

Security Response Team

PROTECTING THE COUNTRY

The U.S. Coast Guard has taken part in many of the armed conflicts that the United States has been involved in. However, the Coast Guard does its main work during peacetime. It enforces all federal laws that relate to maritime activities. The Coast Guard works with other federal agencies to protect the United States from terrorism. It plays a leading role in the fight against **drug trafficking**. The Coast Guard sets up and maintains aids to navigation, such as lighthouses and fog signals. It also does search and rescue work on the seas and saves lives.

The U.S. Coast Guard Reserve supports the Coast Guard. The Reserve can provide personnel and equipment if necessary. Members of the Reserve take the same training as Coast Guard personnel. The U.S. Coast Guard Auxiliary is made up entirely of volunteers. Their main job is to ensure the safety of people who use boats for recreation. The volunteers also help the Coast Guard with search and rescue operations.

On the Front Lines

The U.S. Coast Guard has special forces for maritime situations that threaten the United States and require immediate action. The Maritime Security Response Team rapidly responds to possible terrorist activities. Tactical Law Enforcement Teams combat drug trafficking. Port Security Units protect the nation's ports. The National Strike Force deals with oil spills and hazardous waste clean-up operations. Coast Guard special forces often work closely with the U.S. Navy on their missions.

COAST GUARD CORE VALUES

HONOR Always act with integrity. Take responsibility for your actions. Be honest and always do what you say you will do. Be loyal to Coast Guard and the United States.

RESPECT Treat others fairly. When working with others to reach a common goal, show them respect and do not judge them. This will help get the job done with the best possible results.

DEVOTION TO DUTY Obey Coast Guard rules. Your military duties are more important than your own desires. Put the needs of the troops ahead of your own and have faith in your leaders.

HISTORY OF THE COAST GUARD

The Revenue Cutter Service was created in 1790. A cutter is a government boat used to enforce maritime laws. In 1915, the Revenue Cutter Service combined with the U.S. Life-Saving Service to form the U.S. Coast Guard.

1846 TO 1848
★ Mexican-American War

1917
★ The U.S. enters World War I, which ends the following year

1927
★ Mississippi River flood

1790
★ The Revenue Cutter Service is formed

1812
★ The War of 1812 against Great Britain begins

1861 TO 1865
★ American Civil War

1920 TO 1933
★ Prohibition bans sale of alcohol banned in United States

1915
★ The U.S. Coast Guard is formed

1812

1915

Through the years, the Coast Guard's main work has taken place in the United States and along its coasts. However, the Coast Guard also has supported the other U.S. military branches in armed conflicts in overseas.

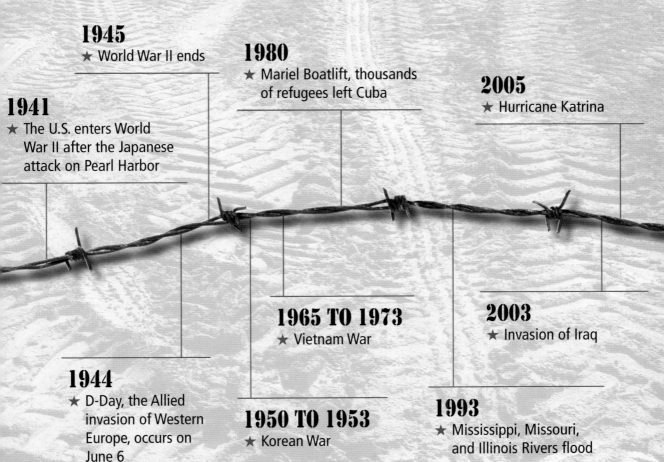

1945
★ World War II ends

1980
★ Mariel Boatlift, thousands of refugees left Cuba

2005
★ Hurricane Katrina

1941
★ The U.S. enters World War II after the Japanese attack on Pearl Harbor

1965 TO 1973
★ Vietnam War

2003
★ Invasion of Iraq

1944
★ D-Day, the Allied invasion of Western Europe, occurs on June 6

1950 TO 1953
★ Korean War

1993
★ Mississippi, Missouri, and Illinois Rivers flood

1945

2005

COAST GUARD BASES AROUND THE COUNTRY

The Coast Guard has a number of facilities on land that support its missions. There are Coast Guard Stations, Coast Guard Air Stations, and Aids to Navigation Stations. There are also several training centers. The Coast Guard Stations and Coast Guard Air Stations are divided into nine districts. Each district is responsible for a different region of the United States.

1 Florida

The U.S. Coast Guard Air Station Clearwater is the Coast Guard's largest air station. The Clearwater station also operates two air stations in the Bahamas. Coast Guard District 7 has its headquarters in Miami, Florida. It is responsible for operations in Florida, Georgia, and South Carolina. It has an especially large fleet of boats and plays a leading role in enforcing U.S. **immigration** laws at sea. This work involves many search and rescue missions because people trying to enter the United States from countries in the Caribbean Sea often sail in poor-quality boats.

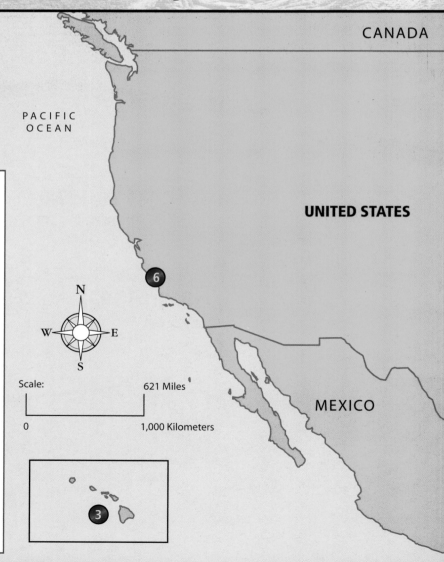

PACIFIC OCEAN

CANADA

UNITED STATES

MEXICO

Scale:

621 Miles

0   1,000 Kilometers

Alabama

The Aviation Training Center in Mobile, Alabama, trains pilots to fly the Coast Guard's helicopters and planes. The Center's air station conducts search, rescue, and homeland security missions. Mobile is also home to the Coast Guard's Gulf Strike Team, an immediate response unit.

Hawai'i

District 14 is the largest Coast Guard district. It has 13 stations across the Hawai'ian Islands. The district also has a station in Japan.

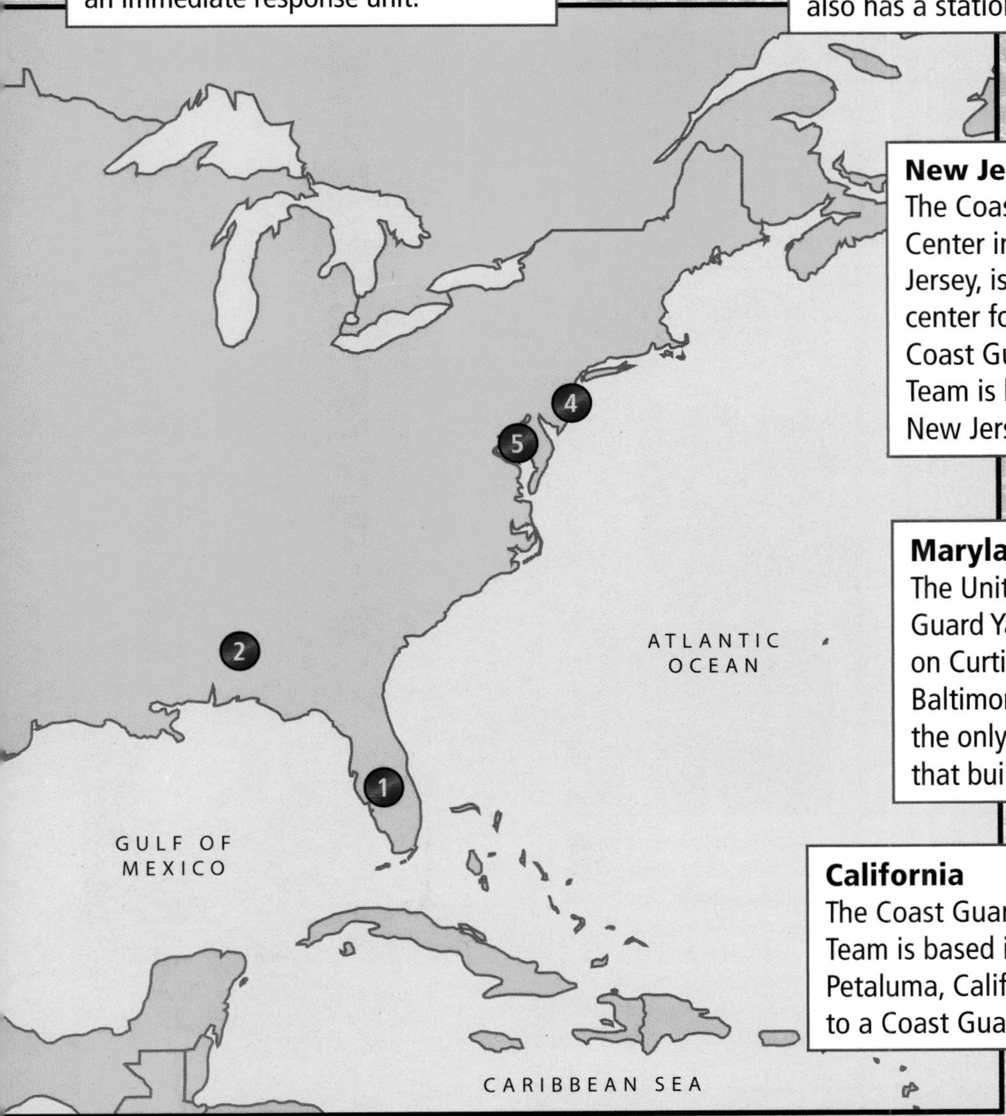

New Jersey

The Coast Guard Training Center in Cape May, New Jersey, is the main training center for new recruits. The Coast Guard's Atlantic Strike Team is based in Fort Dix, New Jersey.

Maryland

The United States Coast Guard Yard is located on Curtis Bay south of Baltimore, Maryland. It is the only Coast Guard facility that builds and repairs ships.

California

The Coast Guard's Pacific Strike Team is based in Novato, California. Petaluma, California, is home to a Coast Guard training center.

ATLANTIC OCEAN

GULF OF MEXICO

CARIBBEAN SEA

COAST GUARD UNIFORMS

The United States Coast Guard has used a number of different uniforms throughout its history.

THE EARLY YEARS

During the late 1800s, sailors in the Revenue Cutter Service wore short pants called pantaloons, tied at the knees. This kept the legs of the pants from getting caught when the sailors worked with the ropes and chains of a ship's masts. Sailors also wore a shirt, a short jacket, and a neckerchief or bandana to use as a sweatband.

Officers in the Revenue Cutter Service had uniforms that were similar to those of the U.S. Navy. The coat was dark blue with gold buttons and lace cuffs. The hat had a wide brim.

Throughout the 1800s, the uniforms of the Revenue Cutter Service changed every so often. In most cases, they closely followed changes in the uniforms of the Navy.

WORLD WAR II

Coast Guard officers wore blue or white dress coats. In warm climates, officers wore tan khaki shorts and shirts when they worked. Khaki is a strong material made from cotton.

In World War II, the Coast Guard uniform for **enlisted personnel** was similar to uniforms worn by Navy sailors. It had a blue pullover shirt called a jumper that was easy to work in. The jumper had a neck flap with white lines around the edge, and one small front pocket without a covering flap. The jumper's cuffs had a white trim. Sometimes there were patches on the sleeve indicating the person's rank. The pants were the same color as the jumper. The hat was flat and had "U.S. Coast Guard" printed on the band.

TODAY

The Coast Guard currently has several different uniforms. Coast Guard personnel wear the Service Dress Blue uniform for business and social occasions. This uniform has a dark-blue jacket with four pockets and blue trousers. The shirt is light blue with two front pockets, and the tie matches the color of the jacket.

The Operational Dress Uniform is the uniform worn by Coast Guard personnel when they are at work. The shirt and pants of the uniform are dark blue. Personnel also wear a baseball-style cap with "U.S. Coast Guard" on it in gold letters.

Coast Guard personnel who do law enforcement and port security work wear the **Camouflage** Utility Uniform. There are different camouflage patterns for different locations and seasons. The desert/summer pattern is tan, brown, and gray, and the woodland/winter pattern is mostly black, brown, and green.

COAST GUARD SHIPS AND AIRCRAFT

THE EARLY YEARS

The first cutters of the Revenue Cutter Service were 10 sailing ships, each about 50 feet (15 meters) in length. Their mission was to combat **smuggling**. They were rugged enough to sail out to sea and withstand severe weather conditions. They also were fast enough to catch the ships used by smugglers. The crews of the cutters were armed with pistols and muskets. Some of the ships had cannons.

THE CIVIL WAR

By the Civil War, the Revenue Cutter Service had begun to use steam-powered cutters. These ships also had sails to use when wind conditions were right. The *Harriet Lane* was one of the best-known cutters. This steamship was about 180 feet (55 m) long and had a paddlewheel as well as sails. It fired the first shot by a ship in the Civil War. This happened at Fort Sumter in South Carolina in April 1861. Later that year, the ship became part of the U.S. Navy's fleet.

WORLD WAR II

The U.S. Coast Guard's most important ships in World War II were the Secretary Class cutters. They were 327 feet (100 m) long. They were fast, dependable, and could operate in a variety of weather conditions. They carried one seaplane and a crew of about 200 members. They were armed with machine guns and anti-aircraft gun systems.

Some cutters accompanied U.S. Navy ships across the Atlantic Ocean during the war. Others patrolled the U.S. coastline. Cutters also supported U.S. military operations in North Africa and Europe, and in the Pacific Ocean.

TODAY

Today, the U.S. Coast Guard uses a variety of ships, boats, aircraft, and weapons. It has about 250 cutters. Cutters are defined as ships more than 65 feet (20 m) long. Cutters can be armed with machine guns and small cannons. They also may have a flight deck for helicopters. The Coast Guard's fleet includes icebreakers, which are used in polar waters and on the Great Lakes. The Coast Guard also has about 1,400 boats under 65 feet (20 m) in length. These are used on lakes and rivers and along seacoasts close to shore.

The U.S. Coast Guard has more than 200 aircraft. Helicopters are based at Coast Guard air stations and on cutters with flight decks. They take part in the fight against smuggling and in rescue operations. Some have guns and armor for protection. Coast Guard planes include the C-130 Hercules and the HU-25A Guardian jet. They are mainly used in operations that take place far from shore.

JOINING THE COAST GUARD

Anyone wishing to join the Coast Guard must be a U.S. citizen or permanent resident. They must be between 17 and 27 years of age and have a high school education. They also are required to pass a medical exam and a test called the Armed Services Vocational Aptitude Battery (ASVAB). Those who wish to become officers can attend the Coast Guard Academy or the Officer Candidate School, both located in New London, Connecticut.

Applying to the Coast Guard

Step One: Talk to a recruiter

Step Two: Talk to family and friends

Step Three: Submit your application

Step Four: Visit the Military Entrance Processing Station (MEPS), where it is determined if you are qualified to join the Coast Guard

OATH OF ENLISTMENT

❝I do solemnly swear that I will support and defend the Constitution of the United States against all enemies, foreign and domestic; that I will bear true faith and allegiance to the same; and that I will obey the orders of the President of the United States and the orders of the officers appointed over me, according to regulations and the Uniform Code of Military Justice. So help me God.❞

Boot Camp Training for Coast Guard recruits is sometimes called Boot Camp. The training takes place at the Coast Guard Training Center in Cape May, New Jersey, and is eight weeks long. It involves physical conditioning drills, swimming, handling weapons, and classes on first aid, fire fighting, and other topics. Recruits also learn all about life in the Coast Guard.

COAST GUARD FACT

The first women to enlist in the Coast Guard were Genevieve and Lucille Baker. They were 19-year-old twin sisters. They enlisted during World War I.

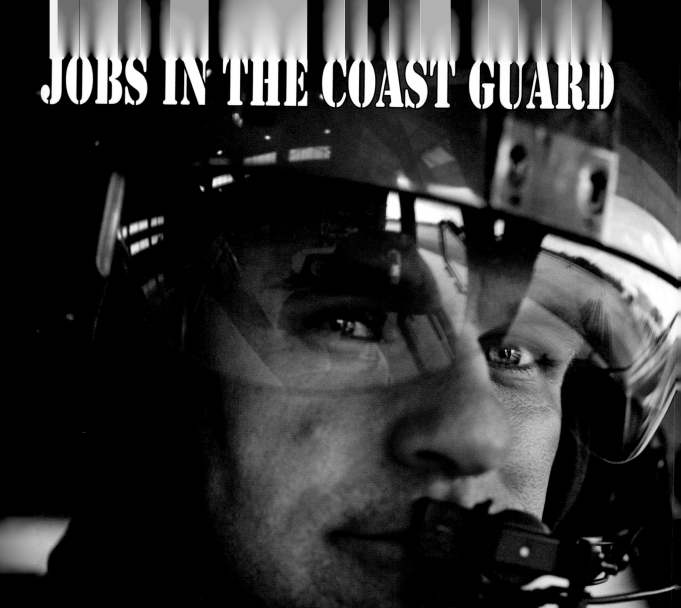

JOBS IN THE COAST GUARD

B eing in the U.S. Coast Guard is not just about serving in combat or law enforcement. There are opportunities to start careers in a variety of fields. There are jobs working with computers and technology, and roles in aviation, electronics, health care, and more. The training and experience gained in the Coast Guard can lead to successful careers in **civilian** life.

Public Affairs

Jobs in public affairs include maintaining good relationships with communications media and the general public. Coast Guard public affairs specialists may write and edit stories about the Coast Guard for newspapers and magazines. They also may represent the Coast Guard at community meetings and press conferences, and on television news shows.

Aviation and Electronics

Work in aviation may involve installing and repairing the electrical, communications, and navigation equipment of aircraft. Jobs in electronics include maintaining and repairing radio receivers and transmitters, radar, and computer equipment.

Marine Science

Coast Guard personnel in this field may investigate incidents that cause water pollution, such as oil spills. They also may supervise the clean-up work and enforce safety regulations to prevent such incidents from happening again. Other jobs involve patrolling ports, inspecting waterfront facilities, and supervising the loading of explosives onto ships.

COAST GUARD COMMUNITY LIFE

In many ways, life in the Coast Guard is much like civilian life. Members of the Coast Guard work regular hours at a job, they spend time with their families, and they fill their free time with hobbies, sports, or any activity they choose.

The Coast Guard's Work-Life Programs provide a wide variety of services to improve the quality of life for families of Coast Guard personnel. These include counseling services, physical fitness programs, and programs to improve education and job opportunities for family members. Other programs provide child care, financial planning services, and help for families to deal with the stress of having a parent working in dangerous situations.

★ Members of the Coast Guard come from all walks of life. Most are on full-time active duty, others work part time, and many serve as volunteers.

WRITE YOUR STORY

If you apply to join the Coast Guard, you will need to write an essay about yourself. This is also true when you apply to a college or for a job. Practice telling your story by completing this writing activity.

1 Brainstorming

Start by making notes about your interests. What are your hobbies? Do you like to read? Are you more interested in computers or power tools? Then, organize your ideas into an outline, with a clear beginning, middle, and end.

2 Writing the First Draft

A first draft does not have to be perfect. Try to get the story written. Then, read it to see if it makes sense. It will probably need revision. Even the most famous writers edit their work many times before it is completed.

3 Editing

Go through your story and remove anything that is repeated or not needed. Also, add any missing information that should be included. Be sure the text makes sense and is easy to read.

4 Proofreading

The proofreading is where you check spelling, grammar, and punctuation. During the proofread, you will often find mistakes that you missed during the editing stage. Always look for ways to make your writing the best it can be.

5 Submitting Your Story

When your text is finished, it is time to submit your story, along with any other application materials. A good essay will increase your chances of being accepted, whether it be for a school, a job, or the Coast Guard.

TEST YOUR KNOWLEDGE

1 When was the Coast Guard founded?

2 How many aircraft does the Coast Guard have?

3 At what age can you apply to join the Coast Guard?

4 Where is the largest Coast Guard Air Station located?

5 Where is Boot Camp for Coast Guard recruits held?

6 What is the uniform that Coast Guard personnel wear for working?

7 How many cutters does the Coast Guard have?

8 What are the three core values of the U.S. Coast Guard?

9 Where is the Coast Guard Academy?

10 What cutter fired the first shot by a ship in the Civil War?

ANSWERS: 1. 1915 **2.** More than 200 **3.** 17 years old **4.** Clearwater, Florida **5.** Cape May, New Jersey **6.** Operational Dress Uniform **7.** About 250 **8.** Honor, Respect, Devotion to Duty **9.** New London, Connecticut **10.** The Harriet Lane

KEY WORDS

camouflage: clothing or other items designed to blend in with the surroundings

civilian: a person who is not an active member of the armed forces

cutter: Coast Guard ships that are 65 feet (20 m) or more in length

Coast Guard Auxiliary: a volunteer workforce that supports the Coast Guard and its activities

Coast Guard Reserve: part-time Coast Guard workforce that can provide personnel and equipment as needed

drug trafficking: buying and selling illegal drugs

enlisted personnel: a member of the Coast Guard below the rank of an officer

immigration: coming to live in a country that is not one's home country

maritime: having to do with the sea

musket: a gun with a long barrel that was used in the past

Revenue Cutter Service: name for the military force that later became the U.S. Coast Guard

terrorism: the use of violence or threats to harm or cause fear within a country

smuggling: to bring things in or take things out of a country illegally

INDEX

Log on to www.av2books.com

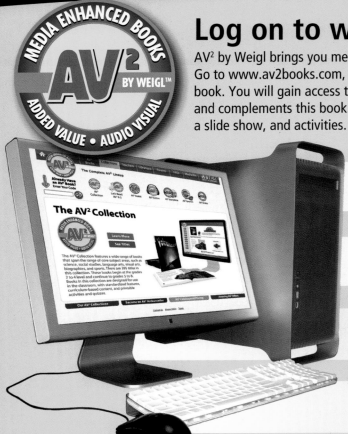

AV² by Weigl brings you media enhanced books that support active learning. Go to www.av2books.com, and enter the special code found on page 2 of this book. You will gain access to enriched and enhanced content that supplements and complements this book. Content includes video, audio, weblinks, quizzes, a slide show, and activities.

Audio
Listen to sections of the book read aloud.

Video
Watch informative video clips.

Embedded Weblinks
Gain additional information for research.

Try This!
Complete activities and hands-on experiments.

WHAT'S ONLINE?

Try This!	Embedded Weblinks	Video	EXTRA FEATURES
Try a timeline activity.	Read about the importance of the Coast Guard.	Watch a video about the Coast Guard.	**Audio** Listen to sections of the book read aloud.
Complete a mapping activity.	Find out more information on the history of the uniform.	Check out another video about the Coast Guard.	
Write an essay about yourself.	Learn more about jobs in the Coast Guard.		**Key Words** Study vocabulary, and complete a matching word activity.
Test your knowledge of the Coast Guard.	Read more information about the Coast Guard.		**Slide Show** View images and captions, and prepare a presentation.
			Quizzes Test your knowledge.

AV² was built to bridge the gap between print and digital. We encourage you to tell us what you like and what you want to see in the future.
Sign up to be an AV² Ambassador at www.av2books.com/ambassador.